The Veronica Maneuver

AKRON SERIES IN POETRY

AKRON SERIES IN POETRY
Mary Biddinger, Editor

Jennifer Moore, *The Veronica Maneuver*
Brittany Cavallaro, *Girl-King*
Oliver de la Paz, *Post Subject: A Fable*
John Repp, *Fat Jersey Blues*
Emilia Phillips, *Signaletics*
Seth Abramson, *Thievery*
Steve Kistulentz, *Little Black Daydream*
Jason Bredle, *Carnival*
Emily Rosko, *Prop Rockery*
Alison Pelegrin, *Hurricane Party*
Matthew Guenette, *American Busboy*
Joshua Harmon, *Le Spleen de Poughkeepsie*
David Dodd Lee, *Orphan, Indiana*
Sarah Perrier, *Nothing Fatal*
Oliver de la Paz, *Requiem for the Orchard*
Rachel Dilworth, *The Wild Rose Asylum*
John Minczeski, *A Letter to Serafin*
John Gallaher, *Map of the Folded World*
Heather Derr-Smith, *The Bride Minaret*
William Greenway, *Everywhere at Once*
Brian Brodeur, *Other Latitudes*

Titles published since 2008.
For a complete listing of titles published in the series,
go to www.uakron.edu/uapress/poetry.

The Veronica Maneuver

JENNIFER MOORE

The University of Akron Press
Akron, Ohio

Copyright © 2015 by Jennifer Moore

All rights reserved • First Edition 2015 • Manufactured in the United States of America. All inquiries and permission requests should be addressed to the Publisher, the University of Akron Press, Akron, Ohio 44325-1703.

19   18   17   16   15   5   4   3   2   1

ISBN: 978-1-629220-29-1 (cloth)
ISBN: 978-1-629220-30-7 (paper)
ISBN: 978-1-629220-31-4 (ePDF)
ISBN: 978-1-629220-32-1 (ePub)

A catalog record for this title is available from the Library of Congress.

∞ The paper used in this publication meets the minimum requirements of ANSI/NISO z 39.48–1992 (Permanence of Paper).

Cover: *Naturaleza Urbana, 2008* by Cecilia Paredes, © 2008. Reproduced with permission. Cover design by Amy Freels.

The Veronica Maneuver was designed and typeset in Stone Print with Futura display by Amy Freels and printed on sixty-pound natural and bound by Bookmasters of Ashland, Ohio.

CONTENTS

I am closer to you
Than land and I am in a stranger ocean
Than I wished
      —Barbara Guest

I heard, could be, a Hey there from the wing,
and I went on:
      —John Berryman

I.

AS A DEBUTANTE I ADJUSTED MY HATPIN

In the year of Our Lord the Electric Chair,
in the year of the Boozehound and the Unhooked Corset,
a lick of salt troubled my tongue.
A lick troubled me into telling the green girls
how to swing from the hundred-footed maple,
and the drowning woman how to sink into the river's bed.
As with all things, the difficulty lies
in making maneuvers look effortless.

In this year of the Obvious Ankles, rouge is applied
with a heavy hand. Cheekbones are achieved
through sucking. Tired of tiny perfumes,
I want to be your *voix de ville*:
watch as I unfurl a web from my wrist.
When it flies, the trapeze artist sets sail;
in each arm, a bunch of begonias. Look how she
tosses her stems to the ushers.

If the sideshow acts fall through—
the moon walkers, the cloud counters—give me a spoon.
I'll be the Depressor of Tongues, the one
to observe every soft palate. The candy-flossing crowd
opens wide, but the stagehand gives me the hook.
Now I play to the haircuts,
the last of the Disappointment Acts.
I'm the tooth that cuts the sucked cheek,
one of a thousand pennies sewn to the vaudevillian's gown.

INSTRUCTIONS FOR GOING UNNOTICED

To disappear, become water. From the faucet
spill out to the sea, then ride in the wake of the whale

'til the ocean is your body and you are the ocean's.
But if evaporation is what you want, pour yourself

from kettle to cup; be sugar and dissolve. Make
saccharine your song and sing it softly. To flee

the observing ear, slip through a needle
and fold quietly into the cabbage rose, unseen

and unsung in a green bed. Be sure to call
yourself *infant,* meaning *unable to speak,*

and as a way of becoming wallflower, paper
your body in paisley and love the corner

that loves you back. Go un-photographed
into the night. Muzzle anything that glows.

[I WENT TO THE CITY, CAME BACK WITH TECHNICOLOR]

I went to the city, came back with Technicolor. I came back
with radio waves and ticket stubs. Lots of ballpoint pens, nothing temporary.

Never wanting all that neon, I dismantled the structure, uncoiled
the blueprints, turned downtown's steel wool into quilting bees

and horse apples. Doesn't each history contain another, possible body?
The husk that could have happened.

Here, we bury our food to keep it cool. We shuck our own corn, just think *night*
and it crops up. Here, repetition is the opposite of digression.

Everywhere, repetition is the opposite of digression. Why is it
all I have are pencils when I want to leave something permanent? Or is what I want

to leave anywhere for good, to never come back—
I was in the middle of a sentence about evening. Even landscape

disintegrates. Do people still take lovers? Who says *lovers* anymore?
What's seductive is the absorption of one image into another: taillights. Box-

cars. Apples in all of my needles' eyes. A bad fever, this drive for departure—
when I come back I will come back as someone's sister,

a little unkempt, lost in a field of corkscrews. Wanting camaraderie,
I will bring a strawberry buckle. Wanting something to unbutton, I will bring

eyeliner, tickets to tonight's game. I will come back, having forgotten
I had ever left. Had ever torn the husk to its quick.

LINES WRITTEN ON A GRAIN OF RICE

If I am carried by fork to the tongue,
I will be carried by tongue to the throat.

Your swallow will single me out:
I'll wait in a pocket of spittle, then fold

into your windpipe's wall. If you cough,
I might multiply; growing there,

I'm the thing that makes you guttural.
The tiniest microscope will reveal

I've embedded myself: a fuzzy burr,
the bit you can't swallow. Surgeons

can repair the heart through the wrist
and through the mouth remove

a kidney, but can they unfasten
the grain from your voice? I'd like

to stay, a sprouting tattoo asleep
in a house I could care for. Inside

your cough, a million coughs
and me, a seed inside a smaller door.

[I SENT MY BLUES AWAY, THEY CAME RIGHT BACK]

I sent my blues away, they came right back.
They came not as single spies, but full battalions
of redcoats, greenhorns, and yellow jackets.
The cavalcade dazzles. My eyes can't take it.

Each lid's done its lidding. Drop a dime on each,
then roll me down the depths of the hallway.
As nail, knob or knocker, Jacob's dead,
but his ghost slips through the doorframe.

About the horror of unlove, he's got a story to tell.
De profundis, but don't believe the hell he depicts.
Nothing bad sticks; even Ebenezer had a way
with women. They say, *You'll get over it*. They say,

Try this: crook your finger, hook her collar,
drag her all the way to Reno. There's something
there to dazzle the loneliest of men;
a pleasure glimpsed through the slit of a skirt.

Thing is, all relocation affords is a chance
to see griefs multiplied tenfold. Dart the rhino,
then airlift her to another jungle. Upside down
and woozy in the sky, every tree's an unknown threat,

and the new landscape's anything but.
Instead I'll stay put, painting the roses red. I'll lie
with the lamb and wait for new hazards to pass.
Only plea: my head is killing me, so tread softly.

SONETTO

Think of the thing that dislocates your ear,
then imagine how the ear is recovered. The blast

and cure, what detonates and mends; and then,
how to restring the instrument. Here the gondoliers

have no need for us; they sing into their own canals
and navigate the city without sinking. Sound

is a form of energy that moves through air and water;
its waves of pressure collect in us. What you want

is char without fuel, *sonetto*, a little song to fill the jar;
you want shaken bottles and sudden explosions.

What I want is your flammable mouth, its cinematic
mottle and cue. We agree to disagree. Gondolier,

navigate the city without poles. Let the little song
and its echo fly through your unfastened ear.

THE VERONICA MANEUVER

It's a difficult day for mercy. Tongues wag, and cash is tossed around. We're in Spain, but it's not the Spain you imagined; the arena's a sawdust stage, a little horror musical. Aficionados make bets. Their cigars trail the opposite of clouds.

While picadors do prep work, we get bored. We peer at the *tercio* through opera glasses and ogle it with our phones. Let's face it: we stare down the lens of whatever at whatever's on display. Above all, we're drawn to the gore of the present.

If I were a bull, I'd have to decide between focusing on a target and charging everything that moves. Either way, I'd get hooked behind the shoulder and brought to my knees in front of everybody. What the spectators want is the *estocada*, the death blow and difficult exit. So banderilleros toss darts into the bull's back; then flowers for the matador, while the body's dragged from the ring. You wear a muleta as a little retro jacket; we pour one out for the bull.

THE CARTOONIST'S DAUGHTER

In the comedy of snapshots, I was backgrounded:
was the wall full of flowers or the saddest lobster in the tank,

which still was somehow funny. In my father's monochrome eye,
in the rough sketch and single panel gag

the girl with the torn stocking was me, Our Darling
of the Smudged Cheeks. The little one who caught the punch-

lines before they hit the trash, and the pencils that fell
from the pockmarked ceiling. But all his comic strips

keep losing their edge; they can't fill enough of this room's balloons
to trigger any sort of chuckle. Writing from inside a garbage can,

I'm waiting for the A-ha! moment, for the Alley-Oop
into real-time laughter—wanting the joke to slip on its own peel

and the eraser to do its job. I am the colorist of muted marvels,
the laugh drawn out and drawn in by his crow quill pen.

INSOMNIAC'S NOCTURNE

When night begins to arrive,
the tiniest joint in the body softens:

delicate as a cuticle, orchid,
or acute as a minute of migraine,

the ear inside your ear
listens for things that adjust

to dimness, that give advice
on how to read them: for sleep,

a tongue's worth of sugar.
Always the milk warm. Lunula

when you need a place to doze,
the moon coming to rest

on a fingernail; then the hazelnut
and its collapsible husks.

And when you want
to be looked after,

when the tangible wire to waking
is severed and nothing is left,

I will be the river, spliced
into three kinds of leaving:

stilled tongue, lip of glass,
the sleeping water sent away.

LINES WRITTEN ON A DROP OF MILK

Call me poise, call me carriage, call me
from the inside of an empty jar—

call me what you want
but when you do, gather me little

by little: I will rest in the cup
of your clavicle or on the tips

of ten fingers; I will land on a tongue
and wander your body's blue note,

the dense marrow or brittle bone—
but if you wring me from your skin,

say I am the thing that falls; call me
a fallen thing and I will go bad,

down the sink's throat; I will
curdle and cloud, go from whole

to evaporate, and then, like that,
to powder—I will go down

and land in the white umbrella
that falls when I fall, will be

a thousand letters in a jar,
the mailbox full of snow.

DOMESTIC STUDY (I)

The house is a curator
of questions, it contains closets

full of board games
In attic light, in door light

she unfolds his notes, opens all
the clothing he folded

She empties the cupboards
of dishes she fills

the cupboards with dust
In bed she is a sentence

he mispronounces
In bed she pulls an orchestra

from out of his mouth
then a pill box full of recipes

For last night's headache
rest a magnet on the temple

or sip from a bottle of
maple syrup

At midnight she builds a room
of spoons she plants a field

of dishes and salt water
To soothe a toothache

place a whole clove between
the jaw and the cheek

Milk for a minor burn
In spoon light, in button light

a pear turns soft
in its bag

a snow globe unlocks from
its wooden foot

some glitter goes missing
the carpets sparkle for a hundred years

SAINT VERONICA HAS SOMETHING TO SAY (I)

El Greco, "St. Veronica with the Holy Shroud," c. 1580

Where Eastern skies shrink away,
and where the Dead Sea swallow
circles the pines, heretics map the blue
and prophesy. They tell us
about constellations,
about floods and invasions,
what will be written and why.
We're told, *Keep quiet,*
but pray for rains to fall.
So raising a cloth to my lips,
I say nothing. I prevent expression
from being seen. But inside,
a tiny whale survives—
a tiny whale in the mouth of a woman—
and between two seas, the poor
walk backwards and forwards.

Dear illegitimates,
I resemble you. Like a veil
hiding nothing, we wail wide.
We wait for the fruit
to be set in our open mouths.
But the city empties out,
and a swallow beats away with my heart.
Imagine me as I imagine you:
as figures walking back
into the book, becoming visible.
Imagine the beached fish
returned to sea—a word
stitched to nothing, then spoken.
Open the door of the lily and walk in.

ON SYMMETRY

Air has no twin: along the sill a film forms,

the window warps: a world translated twice

in glass, a world translated twice, then gone

when the pane clouds over. Without its replica

a thing flails, but adjusts to disparity:

in utero, the vanishing twin vanishing

into clear currency, an ocean swallowed by a sea

and in a blink, the coeval self reimagined

as simply self. When pain clouds the eye,

you see disruption not in a mirror

but as a word—a crab inscription,

a walking between *saw* and *was*.

INSTRUCTIONS FOR CONCHITA CINTRÓN, 1933

To become the Blue-Eyed Torera,
make your first kill in the slaughterhouse.
Jabbing oxen with a dagger will be your drill.
One's eyes must be open to one's own horrors.

One's eyes must be open to one's own performance:
you'll become *diosa rubia*, Blonde Goddess,
the Lady of the Marvelous Wrists. The audience will roar,
but only if you fall in love with the sword.

Art's the act of being carried from one mouth to another;
you must craft pandemonium in the crowd.
It's your *veronicas* that will make it rain carnations.
When you sculpture with the cape, you'll disappear.

Be your own maestro. To the bull, say *I'm the cloud
that taps on your shoulder. When the declining sun shines full,
I make my wrists do marvelous things.* Through her glass eye,
the cat wants the robin's beak, then the entire robin.

So coax the bull closer with a vow: *This blood-dance
will be simulated. As you thunder by, I'll touch your shoulders,
then let my sword drop to the sand.* Be your own maestro.
A clever girl sees through the ruse, not around it.

[WHEN SUNLIGHT BECOMES AN OBJECT]

When sunlight becomes an object, my echo creates a hole in sound:
a thousand doors, many handshakes of air.

Like the snapping hazel flings its yellows into the woods,
my coming and going is marked in the ear of the hearer.

When the hazel dormouse hides, she hides for months at a time.
It's the grip of an unknown animal she fears.

But fear's a tricky thing; at night she shreds the honeysuckle
and builds nests in the crooks of open trees.

If the big-eared bat can sing, then I was that supersonic love song.
Swinging from crag to crag, I was that blind crooning animal.

Like Lorca, I want to sleep the dream of apples.
I want the old dangers to feel welcome—

the wind displacing the fir tree, the fir tree catching on fire.
Let something burn long enough, it'll put itself to sleep.

DISAMBIGUATION: ON DESIRE

For arrest, see Cardiac or Crime. For the place
you'll be taken to, the little place of forgetting, see Oubliette.

See Migraine for a world that weighs inside the brain,
and Bulldozer for a sleep that stays awake.

Hope, or half the bird's bone, is what you'll get
when you arrive at Wish (for the science

of hidden message, see Stenography), and if wishing
doesn't work, try the ancient form of night prayer (Nocturne).

For downpour, see the bin full of Broken Umbrellas;
the wide sky that protects you, Rainshade

or Shadow; that which makes of your body a bull's-eye,
Fusillade. As a last resort, see the one who knows

how to make iron move (Locksmith).
When you're tired of turning pages, he'll tell you love

is a Taiwanese river, an empty seat in Oklahoma, one
of several names for zero. See Heart, see Cardiac, see Arrest.

II.

THE QUIET GAME

I took aim and let the horseshoe go;
it hooked the stake in the sand and landed.
Two dead and three, then three ringers three.
Non-contact sports have their own erotic appeal.

Things That Are Distant Though Near. Things
That Give a Tight Feeling. Things Not Found
Through the Lens of a Telescope
and Visible Only When Blindfolded.

To miss the mark completely
requires its own precision. Lie down,
for instance, shoot a bullet into the sky,
then wait a decade for it to fall to the earth.

Being honest here: those ten years are a bitch.
The bar's closed. We mix our own drinks and draw
our own targets. I make of your body a bull's-eye.
In a series of rifle experiments, nothing was shot,

but the waiting gives a tight feeling. We roll the dice
and move two spaces east. Feet to feet in the grass,
we toss bullets between us. I miss you, you miss me.
We miss each other. A draw makes sense

but ten years later, the shot drops on the lawn.
This late in the game, your neck's the stake for my shoe;
it lands in the sand. Two dead and three, then three
ringers three. Stalemate, standoff. One dead lock.

A wolf carved a hole of a web
on the side of the house and caught moths.
He is a mathematician; he practices addition
and subtraction. In the morning, some things appear

while others vanish. When I cry wolf, I cry spider
and spider, wolf. If I could, for you I'd spin
a whole house of silk from my body,
a mansion carved in the space of a doorjamb.

I envy the spider his sight. He's got eight eyes
to see all things clearly and in every dimension.
If you want to find the mouth of the burrow,
flash a light and look for eye shine. Look for the glint

of a threatened thing. If you want to find my house,
take a left on Locust. There's a porch swing
and bright flowers, but home begins at the trapdoor
in the eaves above the bell. If you cry wolf,

I'll answer as spider; my spider will answer
as me. Every day we eat our own webs
and use our legs to measure distance. We fly
from the sills and shoot intruders. It all sticks.

The spider's tricky. Every morning,
another clingy web to wipe from the siding.
He doesn't want to snag a single bug:
he wants to capture and wrap the whole house.

Of the unopened book: lean forward, bend back,
then break the tight spine. There's a shiver.
Run a thumb along the length of its grain.
Without sex, there's allegory. In this scenario,

the ass and the swallow share a yard. They circle
each other, parting grass with toe and snout.
The swallow says to the ass, *Fight yawn with yawn.*
Ass to swallow: *Lick the inside of your own beak.*

What does the trick's what I say to myself: *Curl the toe,*
then finger the curl. Blindfolded, I quiet down—
if you cover the eyes of the dove, she won't flutter.
Like a good celibate, I ride the cymbal high. I ride it

sidesaddle, then split into astride. *To fill a gap /*
insert the thing that caused it. So I take thumb from mouth;
the swallow sings to spit, then spit sings to swallow.
What does the trick's what the trick does to herself.

In the collected history of listening in
I'm perpetually leaning against the door,
standing in the eavesdrop of your house
and bending my ear to the pillow talk upstairs.

The eye of the needle is narrow
and the peek-space of a keyhole is slim.
You're wearing your suit of apples,
your book's got the broken spine in the den.

In Hundred Fields, Oregon, all the fruit goes bad.
Each time a winter pear drops, I hear you mark
the wall. With my mittened hand, I mark the snow
for every delivered bell and knock.

Around the house I walk softly, I carry a huge ice pick.
I pull my body by the lobe of its waiting ear.
Like asking for pleasure from a pincushion,
I draw every blade you've left in the lawn.

Under the willow tree, willow tree, willow tree
a toad has swallowed the green green fog
The fog has swallowed the mossy shore
The green toad's swallowed the key to my door

Under the willow tree, sleep flies away
the mossy shore swallows the green green wood
In fields full of foxglove, the ladies can't be heard
In fields full of fog, a key closed an open door

Things that can be seen from a boat:
a boy with a hoop, a girl with a yo-yo
the river that slows, the shore that slips away
a dove who cries, who flutters when blind

What to look for in sleep: *Things That Lie in Relation
to Each Other, Things That are Diminished
in Description, Things That Give a Soft Feeling*
The willow tree the willow tree the willow tree

There was a gem in the brain of the acorn,
but the brain of the acorn was squirreled away.
Local boys drew maps of the neighborhood
and told us what to look for. *Things That Want*

to Be Hunted. Things That Give a Weak Feeling.
Things That Should Be Forgotten. In cul-de-sacs
we let doorbells do the work. Neighbors laughed;
the world gave up its tools. Hey, compass:

where do we go for precious things?
Both north and south, up-skirt and down-blouse.
Along the lining of a boot; inside a cat's ear.
When dead ends end, we ask the man with two hearts

how to find the fishermen's moon, and where
the dish goes when it skips town with the spoon.
What he gives us are *Things That Tend to Disappear:*
eye of hibiscus, foxglove in winter. Entire fields of air.

A bee died on the carpet. A bee died
and I vacuumed him up, a whole body gone.
Though it's just an apparatus, a plastic wand,
it's a privilege for the sucker to suck.

On the hardwood floor, there's a wink
you're not supposed to notice; there's a wink
that shouldn't even be there. A button
not doing its job, a button cut from a cuff.

Or it's a button lost from an open blouse.
The wink's not doing its job; its job is to keep
secret things closed. When it fails, there's a flaw
in the eye; a wing and a buzz, a gap in discretion.

When discretion opens, a lily unlocks its jaw,
the Venus catches a fly. The green lip sucks it up.
Down the plush stairs, I scour every step's brim
and draw out the dirt. I polish the floor of scum,

but in the gut's where I gnaw, where the bee body
molders and the button lives for years.
You might as well leave it in the rug. The pin's
the pincushion's pleasure; let it settle in.

If I suggest a toy for you to play with,
close your eyes and choose from the chest.
Be the boy with the hoop, the girl with the yo-yo.
Your chosen treasure will ward off monotony.

Day's not a sieve; it's an altar. You have to sacrifice
the toys of your youth. Toy piano, toy poodle,
toy train. When building a fort, half the fun
comes from destroying your creation.

Rubber duck, paddle ball. With your toy camera, capture
the local girls standing on their heads. We call this game
estrangement; upside down, everything's made to seem odd.
Let the balloon go: it floats to the ground.

Let the infant clutch your finger; she'll hang on
'til she goes down. To grasp blindly is to love.
Everyone knows how the whistle works: purse your lips
and blow. Everyone knows the core of the balloon is air.

You be the canary, I'll be the coal. In this scenario
the canary has nothing to say; its feathers
become less yellow. The mine yawns. It opens
and closes on dark. What the coal says, goes,

but the feathers want their yellow back. They yell
for it. They yell for it. The yawn returns and closes
on the light. Yellow can speak for itself. The mine
closes on the bird, but regrets its own methodical dark.

When you say you'll be the tar, I say I'll play the pit.
What the pit wants, the pit gets. When I say
you're me, you say I'm you. Rubber, glue.
When the canary croons, it doesn't croon for you.

The bird clings to its yellow, but under dark
you become coal, not mine, and the coal has nothing
to say. The coal has nothing to say. What's yours
is mine and mine is yours. You the coal, the canary me.

In the space of time it takes for an eyelash to grow,
I hitched my wagon to a star and took off.
Easting and westing, northing and southing,
I toured the silver ruins of an all-night sky.

Past the controlled burn of the meteor,
past Wynken and Nod's little shoe—
but the orbit slows; my wagon's star drops.
I miss the sea, how it rids itself of noise:

the spray of the great blue whale, the white-
tipped notes passed from Water to Air.
I remember how the golden broom grows
on the beaches, how the beaches are blown bare.

Back and forth, and back and forth, the broom
plays a game with the land all day—it's called
Turn Aside, then Charm, then Draw Away.
For four players: Sand, Wind, Ocean, and Sky.

You are a pool of oil, very calm   Very still
and very calm on the cool and cooling floor
I slip around the edges; the edges creep in
An animal, I creep until you gather up and go

I like the stone wall, it does its job   It doesn't move
for fifty years   For a hundred years, the wall waits
regarding sun   absorbing wind   It waits
for things to happen   Which do or do not occur

People say, *Don't run with the blade*   People say
Cut away from the body, sew away from those
who hold the cloth   I could do that   I could, but
people forget to say   *The last stitch is through the nose*

III.

THE GALLERY OF UNRECOVERABLE OBJECTS

Welcome, *voyeur*, to the Gallery of Unrecoverable Objects.
You derive your pleasure from looking? We'll sate your need for novelty.

As curator I'll give you flash and flair, but unlike the magpie,
I'll withdraw all inflection from the giving.

Follow the arrows on the floor, etched with ancient pencils. Disregard
the broom-tailed dogs that sniff our every move; they'll sweep away

the crumbs you've dropped for those who'd seek you out.
Do not observe the wallflower as we pass. Her fear of strange faces is crippling,

and though she's well secluded among vines, she will not last the night.
Now look both ways down the Corridor of Infinite Regress. At one end

you'll see the landlocked lighthouse, replicated in our mirrored walls; at the other,
elephant garlic on parade. And here is the Famous Poet, nailing an egg to the floor.

Do not mind the Poet, for it is his duty to fasten his goods to the ground.
The floor will yield to his nailing; the egg will not.

Gentlemen, Ladies, the Great Hall of Historical Poems
is closed for maintenance. So, too, the Hall of Half-Finished Crosswords,

Faulty Soufflés, and Unforwarded Mail. And here lies the Failed Poet:
she had a happy childhood, but her soups lacked salt. Her epitaph reads,

You caught me mid-wink, dear reader. Watch as I put on my fascinator.
If you desire Golden Advice, seek, out of better books, wisdom.

Patrons, the Famous and the Failed Poet are one. See how they lean
on the fixed arm of the sewing machine? They wear the treadle out.

If, like children, you fear what you've seen, take the stairs. You'll have nowhere
to go but up, but don't agonize over the trail you've left;

it will be doggedly swept, the arrows washed away in the rain. It will be as if
you were never here, were one of many lenses dialed back into the telescope.

HAUTE COUTURE GROTESQUE, OR
TALKING ABOUT MY GENERATION

After the mild war, the war that seemed to only last an hour,
we noticed many different kinds of sky. Each advertised

its own demise: one atomic, one apocalyptic, another ironic.
We learned to live with it. Here in the Year of the Bore,

the Year of the Stethoscope, we are told the weather will go
from balmy to brutal in twelve hours flat. We are told

It's a miniature winter, but it's a winter that keeps on happening;
it's one long cough on the way to April. Our lungs are their own

carcinogens. Some of us subscribe to the Chicken Noodle diet
while the rest swear by Wonder Bread, the vodka-cigarette

method, the Quaker Oats technique. We are told *Try to get*
some sleep. In retaliation, we hit the town and make requests:

I'll have a Greyhound, a Scotch and soda. I'll have a double Sazerac.
Despite the drop in egg count, we are forever photogenic:

we've found a way to bottle the juice of the pomegranate,
we know all sorts of synonyms for *stimulus*.

Though the view from the rooftop's spectacular,
we've evolved past our need for eyes. We're hoping

the skies will implode after last call, that we can still
hear the weather, that someone will tell us what to expect.

AS A CHILD OF TWELVE, I BURIED A BOX

As a child of twelve, I buried a box
under the silver claw of the jungle gym.
The sawdust, the rocks; an impulse to hide.
We all said no secrets, right? I lied.

Inside I placed a snow globe, a fortune cookie
and a letter to my future self. It read, "Dear Jen,
We live at the end of the Loneliest Road
in the West. Wind turns the bristlecone red;

the Hotel Nevada blinks from miles away.
In our house, a piano plays itself. Pillows shout.
How old are you now? I wish I was your age."
Let's pity the kid who pines for twenty more years.

Scratch that. Pity or praise the girl who wishes
for ten millennia—she'll end up heading back
to find her capsule. Helmeted and stylish,
at warp speed in a flying saucer, I land.

In the act of digging, the claw wags a finger.
I wag back. But I hit a snag: the landscape's a mess.
Mount Moriah cries in lava; lava cries in gas.
Where there's smoke—you know the rest.

Before the claw curls into a fist, I split. Despite
my mantra—*Reveal yourself, microscopic world!*—
all I took was my cookie and crushed fortune.
It read, *When it becomes difficult*

to think of the space of ten thousand years,
think of the snow globe. Its water serves
as a medium through which glitter falls,
but somebody else always does the shaking.

LINES WRITTEN ON THE BACK OF A TOOTH

Look, here. Wisdom is wanting. On a clear day,
anchor the mirror, then anchor two. Don't chew.

With a tongue, probe the groove. Nudge the bud
'til it throbs, then drag yourself to the waiting room.

In order to excise the molar gone wrong,
the expert will put you under. Not quite the sting

of the acacia ant; nobody's fired a staple
through your cheek. No one's dropped a red coal

on your tongue, then forced the jaw shut.
On the contrary: all at sea, the thing you'll feel

feels like nothing at all. Wait while he grabs
the neck of the tooth, drills the maple

and drains the sap. After the pluck,
you're barely able to part pith from flesh.

A fog will befuddle your moves.
Draw carefully from the scoop of a spoon;

be sure not to suck. When the reasoning brain
returns, you'll come back, too,

but I'm the bit you'll be missing.
Slipped between pillowcase and pillow,

I'll be carried away by the fairies;
a yellow clench under a cushion,

with one wish—*Little prison, little mouth,*
let me find a way to enclose you.

HELLO, GOODBYE

When nothing began, you tethered yourself to the East
and let the ball fly. You let mileage do the work of pointing a finger

and squaring a jaw. More or less, you're the din

in my hard-of-hearing ear, while the other's pressed against
this decade's sure crib. Hear that? A baby cries

through someone else's monitor. A baby cries through

another radio, someone turns a corner
down. A page listens. How the night clears up

isn't clear at all—it's not a logic that gets us, but the wick

of a feeling. If I had something to say, it would be this:
Come outside with me, but ignore the moon.

GHOST LIMB

At night,
the marrow chirps: a woodpecker
        descends: the tendons

twitch. Tickle, scythe, phantom itch.

Bone gone, the memory is limbed
        for years,

root weight without the flesh.

In the small hours
        I call out:

Bird, loosen your beak from my knee.

CENTO: BUT I, BEING YOUNG AND FOOLISH

But I, being young and foolish, against the verge of sky
      as other sadnesses fall across the democracy of objects,

I, being young and foolish,
      haul to the tip of your tongue and I look and look:

the troubled robins, once more in the handkerchief trees
      create a hurt that whispers;

grief brought to numbers, and the storm
      clouds the light, where the water hardly moves.

In my doorway with nothing to say,
      being young and foolish, I look and look:

sitting alone with your tea and your crime,
      there's a light in your eye that keeps.

And then the winter's long,
      then it's longer than afterwards,

and I, being young and fretful
      waited for you to fall into admirable fooling.

How strange, how I've mistaken you for somebody else,
      somebody to slip into my shirt at dusk

and be the heart's boat. I am two fools, I know,
        for loving, and for saying so.

I want to part company with the storm,
        the congenital heartbreak, purge sea water's fretful salt away;

but the emotion is, after all, an artfully conjured gesture
        and seems, briefly, to be a fire escape.

Come along, Fool, it's on the tip of your tongue:
        loosen up your magic, be the heart's boat.

How strange, how, being young and foolish,
        I am for all waters, with nothing to say.

What's true of oceans is true, of course, of poems:
        you'll drown, dear. You'll drown.

'Tis a naughty night to swim in;
        this pitch of tenderness will turn us all to fools.

I WENT AND CAUGHT A FALLING LEAF

I went and caught a falling leaf, then tore it up and cried.
Poor Margaret! they say. *She sees herself in the trash of a tree!*
It's true. I panic, and become the tiny pharaoh ant.
It's his job to build, then destroy, an empire from detritus.

Spring of the leaf, and fall of the leaf. The earth breathes in,
then out, then in again. I learned that in Biology 101.
But my knowledge bores me. To entertain the local boys,
I read from forbidden books. *The Invention of the Diphthong,*

Sword-Swallowing and Its Effects. We learn nothing
except how to tongue-thrust with gusto. That's where
the fun begins. Whole afternoons are shot to hell, spent
touching tip to tip. You know how that goes. Not well.

The hippopotamus yawns to intimidate his rival; I yawn
to put off my lover. It rarely works. Instead, I play dead
and, like the mannequin, know how to sell my stuff.
I pay for boudoir photos with proceeds from my latest book,

Seduction for Dummies. Three cheers for Margaret; of detritus,
she made empire! But sales are slow. Months go by.
To soothe the sting, I roll my wasted effort into a dozen balls,
then stuff them into the mouths of mummified crocodiles.

Now we're all yawning. Touching tip to tip, I fashion
a life from spit and guess the ghost with my eyes closed.
Under tree litter, someone breathes out, someone else
breathes in. It's true; the mannequin mourns for you.

DOMESTIC STUDY (II)

She rips ragweed out by the root

and predicts all the bad weather. She knows
what to wait for: she listens for snow

and when it falls, she lets her hair down

lock by lock. She untucks her blouse
and wonders what ought to show. Under

her breath she'll say your name,

then light the stove and let the kettle go.
She used to hide under sheeted chairs

and count clouds which evolved

from her thinking; she thought her thought
until the sky spilled frostbite. Now

she rubs snow on skin and applies butter

to the bruise; she cares for minor burns
with honey and gauze. At night she draws

a bath and drags a nail along the tub.

She puts her hand there and draws circles
on the window. She puts her hand there.

She lets her hand stay. You think she is

a print ghosting the glass, but you're wrong:
she is the air that gets into your lungs

and the surgeon of your branched

breath. The sugar cane that slips
into the brain. A wind reminding itself

of sleep, she'll drag the river away from its bed.

OH INCOGNITO

We who don't know
what to call ourselves

look to the West
for new temperatures.

Some endless Idaho winter
decides to arrive

in thin light disguised
as a wool dress:

dilapidation
in a word, and you

breaking the bones
of the fish with your teeth.

At night
we find our voices

in boxes of snuff;
we wrap the limb in gauze

before the wound
knows what to call itself.

AND DID IT ALL GO

Leave a note pinned
to the lampshade tell me

where you've been
resting, tell me where

in resting
your hair has fallen

apart—
in the folds

of your thinned sleeve or
along the curve

of a thorn
and then tell me how

to let this salt go
from its ceiling of air

how to unfasten these
buttons and tell me what

can you say to an evening
that never leaves

OUR LADY OF THE MARVELOUS WRISTS

Conchita Cintrón, 1949

I killed my first kill in the slaughterhouse.
Stabbing oxen with a dagger was my drill.
One's eyes must be open to one's own horrors.

One's eyes must be open to one's own persona:
with training I became the Blue-Eyed Torera,
diosa rubia, the Blonde Goddess of the Arena.

I fell in love with a sword, then made pandemonium
in the crowd. Through her glass eye, the cat
wants the robin's beak, then the entire robin.

Bull, I'll be the cloud that taps on your shoulder.
When the declining sun shines full in your eyes,
my wrists do marvelous things.

It's my *veronicas* that dazzle the afternoon
and make it rain carnations in the ring.
The audience roars: "Bait the bull, you bait me."

So let me coax you closer, but: this blood-dance
will be simulated. As you thunder by, I'll touch
your shoulders, then drop my sword in the sand.

The death-blow will not be remembered.
When I sculpture with the cape, I disappear.
A clever girl peeks through the door, not around it.

SAINT VERONICA HAS SOMETHING TO SAY (II)

We speak of killing a trout with a rod. It is the effort made by the trout
that kills it.
—Ernest Hemingway

If what I tell you is true, the pain inside your jaw will not abate.
The absorber and the absorbed become one.

Caught in a quarantine, the jaw says to the hurt
You're my voice now. It has learned the art of ventriloquism,

the art of making another mouth move.
But come close, I have something to tell you:

the caught fish can unhook its lip
and reenter the water. If what I say is true,

knives sharpen themselves and wait for meat.
Ice can thaw from the inside out.

AFTER ALL THAT, THERE IS THIS

To the great sea of Forlorn, we traveled
our goodbye. The water waves.

Beach parsley, switch grass.
I button myself inside your shirt.
You're somewhere else,

a vast heart, caught in the trees.

How your hands know things:
the sounds I didn't make

gathering my hair—
a soft argument, spiraling—

There's never new weather, the water says. We wave back.

NOW YOU SEE IT, NOW YOU DON'T

First, the scene of the crime is drawn. Then the body lies down in its chalk.

"You knew what you were getting into" is something people say, after the fact.

One way to heal a heart is to remove the offending thorn. To prove himself to his audience, Houdini swallowed a series of needles, then pulled them from his mouth, threaded together on a single string.

Nix on memory, though: it hides. Name of the game. As soon as we try to conjure last August, it's gone. We replace its sting with another red lantern, then go for it all over again.

I try to believe that the rain gives as much as it takes, that the thorn in the thumb does as much good as ill. Magician to audience: "Belief's an enemy of fact."

What's that game where you blindfold someone, then spin them around? In the future, there will be no more sympathy for fools. But every senseless thing travels in clouds, escaping the eye.

IN THE DRAWER OF MY WOODEN PILLOW, I FOUND A LEAF

In the drawer of my wooden pillow, I found a leaf.
From it I made eight leaves, stitched a spine, and turned it into a book.

I call it the Folio of Replicated Sounds. Like the lyrebird
who hangs his music in my head, I mimic what I hear:

B is for bullhorn and bacchanalia, H is for the human sob.
For the laughing song of the kookaburra, turn to K,

and for the decibel level of the male moan, M.
But it is the Leaf-Turning Month. I close my book and pluck

from the alder a twig; I remove its pith with a needle
and line the body with graphite. A thought like a bolt of cloth

unrolls, and I scrawl it through the air: "If the dogwood flower's
not a flower, and the lyrebird apes both cricket and kettle,

then I'll play all of the above: the leaf posing and the flower it surrounds,
the bird and the chirp and the whistle." But the range of resonance

is much too much: each murmur and zing turns my book into
the tiniest Ark, a mass masquerade that implodes in a structural collapse—

so I un-stitch the spine, sew eight leaves into one,
and deeper than sound could ever dive

I drown my book in its own noise. In my wooden pillow,
the pasture's all standstill. In my wooden pillow, it's raining only rain.

NOTES

"As a Debutante I Adjusted My Hatpin" is based on the vaudeville performer Eva Tanguay.

The Saint Veronica poems take as their subject the "pious matron of Jerusalem" who, according to Christian legend, accompanied Jesus Christ on the road to Calvary and offered him her veil to wipe his face. Medieval paintings of Veronica primarily show a woman holding up a cloth revealing an image of Christ's face; it's from this context we get the "veronica maneuver" in bullfighting, a technique the matador uses to draw the bull with his cape.

"Instructions for Conchita Cintrón, 1933" and "Our Lady of the Marvelous Wrists" concern Cintrón, a Peruvian bullfighter whose penultimate fight in Spain in 1949 was quite notorious. As Spain did not allow women to approach the bull on foot, Cintrón requested permission to do so and make the final kill; her request was denied. She prepared for the act anyway, then dropped her sword in front of the bull, symbolically touching it on both shoulders to signify success. Cintrón was arrested following the fight, but due to the crowd's overwhelming support for her, was immediately released. The phrase "marvelous wrists" is from Ernest Hemingway's *Death in the Afternoon*.

Parts of "The Quiet Game" are reworkings, riffs or direct transcriptions of material from Oscar Wilde (*The Picture of Dorian Gray)*, Sei Shōnagon *(The Pillow Book)*, John Ashbery ("Paradoxes and Oxymorons"), Emily Dickinson ("To fill a gap—" (546)), Ezra Pound (*Collected Letters*), Sappho ("Do you remember//How a golden/broom grows"), Bram Stoker (*Dracula*), and Samuel Barber ("Under the Willow Tree," from *Vanessa)*.

"Cento: But I, Being Young and Foolish" includes text from John Donne's "The Triple Fool," Cornelius Eady's "I'm a Fool to Love You," James Galvin's "Fool's Errand," Jewel's "You Were Meant for Me," Led Zeppelin's "Fool in the Rain," Pavement's "Easily Fooled," Phosphorescent's "Nothing was Stolen," D.A. Powell's "Callas Lover," Cat Power's "Fool," William Shakespeare's *King Lear* and *Twelfth*

Night, Jack Spicer's "Any fool can get into an ocean…," and W.B. Yeats' "Down by the Salley Gardens."

"Oh Incognito" takes its title from Emily Dickinson's "Good night, because we must" (114).

ACKNOWLEDGMENTS

Many thanks go out to the editors of the following journals, in which some of these poems, at times in earlier versions, appeared:

American Letters & Commentary: "Cento: But I, Being Young and Foolish"
Barrow Street: "Ghost Limb"
B O D Y: [When sunlight becomes an object]
Burnside Review: "The Cartoonist's Daughter"
Cleaver Magazine: "Our Lady of the Marvelous Wrists"
Columbia Poetry Review: "Instructions for Going Unnoticed"
failbetter: [A wolf carved a hole of a web], [If I suggest a toy for you to play with], [You are a pool of oil, very calm]
Fugue: "Disambiguation: On Desire," "Lines Written on a Grain of Rice"
Handsome: "Domestic Study (II)"
Inter/rupture: "In the Drawer of My Wooden Pillow, I Found a Leaf"
Jet Fuel Review: "Hello, Goodbye"
Juked: "Haute Couture Grotesque, or Talking About My Generation"
Kettle Blue Review: "And Did It All Go," "Instructions for Conchita Cintrón, 1933," "Lines Written on the Back of a Tooth"
The Literary Bohemian: [I went to the city, came back with Technicolor]
Natural Bridge: "Sonetto"
Newfound Journal: [In the space of time it takes], [Of the unopened book], [Under the willow tree], [You be the canary, I'll be the coal]
The MacGuffin: "Lines Written on a Drop of Milk," "Oh Incognito"
Mad Hatter's Review: [I sent my blues away, they came right back]
Memorious: "The Veronica Maneuver"
Phantom Limb: [In the collected history of listening in], [There was a gem in the brain of the acorn]
Pinwheel: [I took aim and let the horseshoe go]
RHINO: "Saint Veronica Has Something to Say (II)"
Salt Hill: "As a Child of Twelve, I Buried a Box"
Transom: "Domestic Study (I)," "On Symmetry"

TYPO: "I Went and Caught a Falling Leaf"
Volta: [A bee died on the carpet]
West Branch: "Insomniac's Nocturne"

[A bee died on the carpet] appeared in *Winged: New Writing on Bees.*
"As a Debutante I Adjusted My Hatpin" appeared in *Best New Poets 2012.*

Abundant thanks to my teachers, past and present, who made this book possible: Christina Pugh, Anne Winters, Jennifer Ashton, Mark Canuel, Elizabeth Robinson, Peter Michelson, Jeff Roessner, Heidi Hosey, and Heather Matheson. To my dear friends, who supported its emergence in so many ways, much gratitude: Anthony Madrid, Matthew Corey, Virginia Konchan, Brian Dickson, Simone Muench, Scott Wollschleger, Sara Hunt, Beth McDermott, Jenny Morse, Erin Rice, and Patrick Thomas. To the editorial team at the University of Akron Press, many thanks—especially the fantastic Mary Biddinger for selecting this book and championing it tirelessly, and Amy Freels for her beautiful design sense. The most love, always, to my family, to Diz, and to Jeff—more today than yesterday.